Spanish-American
Blanketry

A special publication in celebration
of the eightieth anniversary
of the School of American Research

Spanish-American Blanketry

Its relationship to aboriginal weaving in the Southwest

H. P. Mera

With an Introduction by Kate Peck Kent
and a Foreword by E. Boyd

School of American Research Press   Santa Fe, New Mexico

School of American Research Press
Post Office Box 2188
Santa Fe, New Mexico 87504-2188

Editor: Jane Kepp
Designer: Deborah Flynn Post
Typographer: Casa Sin Nombre
Printer: Dai Nippon Printing Co.

Library of Congress Cataloging in Publication Data:

Mera, H. P. (Harry Percival), 1875-1951.
   Spanish-American blanketry.

   1. Hand weaving—Southwest, New—History.
2. Blankets.   I. Title.
TT848.M47   1987   746.9'7'089680789   87-12879
ISBN 0-933452-21-7
ISBN 0-933452-22-5 (pbk.)

Contents

Acknowledgments

The School of American Research would like to thank the following organizations and individuals who so generously supported the publication of this book: the International Folk Art Foundation, Santa Fe, New Mexico; the Spanish Colonial Arts Society, Inc., in honor of Mr. and Mrs. John Gaw Meem; the James Russell Agency; Suzanne Baizerman; Fred Boschan; Dr. and Mrs. J. J. Brody; Gilbert and Alice Bucknum; Kenneth S. Clark; Mr. and Mrs. Robert P. Coffin; James T. Crow; Dr. Edward B. Danson; Mr. and Mrs. James H. Duncan; Dr. and Mrs. Greg Gordon; Edward T. and Mildred Reed Hall; Mr. and Mrs. Duane Humlicek; David W. Irving; Mrs. Eugene Kingman; Prof. Orville Linck; Lois R. Livingston; Mrs. John Gaw Meem; Mrs. H. E. Merrill; Lois J. Minium; Mr. and Mrs. Gordon Pettit; Gloria F. Ross; Mr. and Mrs. Luke Vortman; David A. Wenger; Samantha W. and John T. Williams; Dr. Stephen Williams; and Dr. and Mrs. Richard Woodbury.

An Introduction to Mera's Manuscript
Kate Peck Kent

Dr. H. P. Mera commenced his research on Spanish-American weaving at the beginning of the twentieth century, a time of little information and many misconceptions about the art. He had completed a manuscript on the subject by the late 1940s, only a few years before his death in 1951. The School of American Research (SAR) prepared the book for publication in 1965, setting type and making color transparencies for twenty-four plates, but a shortage of funds kept the book from being printed, and it was consigned to the SAR archives. It has since been consulted by a few students of Spanish-American weaving as a starting point for their research. E. Boyd referred to the manuscript in *Popular Arts of Spanish New Mexico*,[1] as did several authors in *Spanish Textile Tradition of New Mexico and Colorado*, edited by Nora Fisher.[2] It is now published here for the first time.

The history of the early Spaniards in the Rio Grande Valley had not been completed when Mera wrote, explaining a few errors and lacunae in his book. His most serious mistake is dating the introduction of the treadle loom—or flat, horizontal harness loom, as he calls it—to about A.D. 1750, or somewhat more than a hundred years later than we now believe it to have occurred. We know that Juan de Oñate and his colonists, arriving in 1598, brought no loom parts or weaving tools with them and depended on the Pueblos' annual tribute of mantas to supplement their clothing needs, as Mera describes. However, less than forty years after Oñate's arrival, woven goods were being produced on treadle looms for trade to Chihuahua. Mera records a 1638 trade invoice listing nineteen pieces of *sayal*, each about one hundred meters long, which could only have been woven as yard goods on treadle looms with cloth and yarn beams capable of holding such lengths. It is a matter of record that by that time, Governor Luís de Rosas had established an *obraje*, or workshop, in Santa Fe, employing captive Apaches and Utes and perhaps some Pueblos as weavers. He was accused of seizing "looms owned by private citizens in order to give his own workshop a greater monopoly over local textile production."[3]

---

[1]Museum of New Mexico Press, Santa Fe, 1974.
[2]Museum of New Mexico Press, Santa Fe, 1979.
[3]Ibid., p. 193.

As Mera points out, "Pueblo weaving would seem to have no direct relationship with the development of the Rio Grande blanket," but not, as he assumes, because Rio Grande Pueblos had ceased to weave in the 1700s and so could not affect Spanish artisans. The weaving of clothing for domestic use continued in some of the Pueblo villages through the nineteenth century, although many people turned to the western Pueblos to supply their needs.

That the weaving of neither the Rio Grande Pueblos nor the western Pueblos influenced Spanish textiles in any way is an interesting fact explained by a number of factors. For one thing, Pueblos principally wove articles of traditional clothing in a style quite different from that of the Spaniards. After the Spaniards brought their own looms, they could weave blankets to their own tastes rather than using Pueblo-style mantas. For another, the looms of the two groups were geared to produce different kinds of textiles: to weave a Spanish-style blanket on a Pueblo loom is feasible enough, but it is not possible to produce a Pueblo manta with decorative end borders on a narrow treadle loom. Finally, the traditional Pueblo weaver was a man working in a kiva, removed from public view, which would have discouraged exchange of ideas between Pueblos and Spaniards.

None of the research on dyestuffs reported in Fisher's 1979 publication[4] was available to Dr. Mera, so he speaks of dyes in the terms generally current in his time and indeed until the late 1970s. He assumes yellow to have been extracted from *chamiso* (*chamisa*, or rabbit brush). This is one common source of yellow used by handloom weavers in New Mexico for generations, but it was not identified as the dye in any of the twelve samples of yellow tested by Max Saltzman and reported in *Spanish Textile Tradition of New Mexico and Colorado.*[5]

Mera and other writers speak of logwood (Campeche wood) and brazilwood as one dye, the source of the reddish brown color distinctive in one type of Spanish-American striped blanket. In fact, logwood yields black, blue, purple, and silver-gray, but not reddish tones, and is quite distinct from brazilwood.[6] Saltzman found no brazilwood in the Rio Grande blankets he tested, one of which is that illustrated here in Plate 2. He does state that the reddish browns may be from a closely related red dye wood.[7] Red in the three-ply imported yarn referred to by Mera in the caption to Plate 4 proved to be cochineal, as did three-ply red yarns in the cotton blanket illustrated in Plate 13.

Mera uses the term "tapestry" for what is currently spoken of as "weft-faced" weave, which simply means that the wefts are battened tightly together to obscure the warps of a fabric. Weft-faced plain weave was the standard technique for Rio Grande banded-pattern blankets. Plain weave tapestry, a technique in which discontinuous wefts of different colors build a pattern of geometric or floral motifs, is the technique used in Mera's "hybrid style" blankets and other figured pieces. Also, when he states

---

[4]Ibid., pp. 207–220.
[5]Ibid., p. 214.
[6]Ibid., p. 209.
[7]Ibid., pp. 213–214.

that "the colonial blanket weaver seems never to have attempted any sort of twilling," he is speaking solely of blankets, knowing perfectly well that *jerga*—the coarse yardage used for clothing, sacks, and floor coverings—was usually woven in twill on the treadle loom.

Finally, Mera's description of double-woven blankets is confusing and incorrect. Trish Spillman, in *Spanish Textile Tradition of New Mexico and Colorado,*[8] explains the process accurately. Double-woven blankets are almost all weft-faced plain weave patterned by simple weft stripes, Mera's "early striped style." It is the blankets woven in two pieces and then sewn together that are more elaborately designed.

Dr. Mera concluded his study in the 1940s, when he saw the weavers producing for the tourist trade blankets and other articles that bore little resemblance in design or quality to the fine old nineteenth-century Rio Grande textiles. He wrote that "attempts to duplicate anything like the achievements of the past are apparently destined to prove unavailing. . . . All the efforts to accomplish this have thus far come to naught." Instead, since about 1970, there has been a revival of interest in nineteenth-century textile traditions, and a number of Spanish artisans are weaving blankets of great beauty, the designs inspired by the work of their ancestors. For a good account of Hispanic textile production in twentieth-century New Mexico, see the chapter by Charlene Cerny and Christine Mather in *Spanish Textile Tradition of New Mexico and Colorado.*[9]

Despite these minor shortcomings, Mera's work offers an excellent picture of the blankets woven by Spanish-Americans in the Rio Grande Valley in the nineteenth century. He is the first scholar to have recognized their beauty and historic importance, and the first to show definitively that they are wholly Spanish, owing nothing in technique or design to the Pueblo weaving that preceded the Spaniards and their looms in the Southwest. His remarks on the influence of Navajo design on Spanish weavings of the 1870s and 1880s are particularly insightful. He describes clearly the "class of loomwork" popularly called Chimayo weaving that developed after about 1900 in and near the village of Chimayo, and he distinguishes it from nineteenth-century Rio Grande weaving. *Spanish-American Blanketry* is indeed a valuable contribution on a little known subject, remarkably complete for its time and still useful to scholars and others interested in Spanish colonial arts.

---

[8]Ibid., p. 58.
[9]Ibid., pp.168–190.

Foreword

Among the many admirable qualities of Dr. Harry Mera's personality were a lively interest in human motivations and a conviction that nameless craftsmen had good and practical reasons for making certain things in a certain way in addition to those catchalls of "ceremonial tradition" so often cited as governing the handiwork of the anonymous makers. In his sometimes exhaustive research into the "why" as well as the "how," he became, inevitably, aware of the impacts of culture contacts which, although unrecorded in writing, were clearly reflected in the inanimate objects under his scrutiny.

In the field of Spanish-American blanketry he was a pioneer. Unlike some of his contemporaries, Dr. Mera saw the slow and often painful adjustment of aboriginal Indian and colonial Spaniard as factual history rather than as a romantic saga of heroes and villains. The background of three hundred years of these mutual social adjustments served him as a guide in research on the non-Indian textiles of New Mexico. Newcomers to the state had forgotten, or never knew, that in the past both Spanish and Indians had been weavers. In the separation and identification of their two styles to students and collectors, he won recognition of the Rio Grande blanket, as he so logically named it, as a class of regional textile worthy of notice in its own right. Variations in design elements over a century, he found, reflected exposure to exotic influences. These, like a true hunter, he took keen pleasure in tracking down from such widely scattered sources as Lancashire, Saxony, and Mexico. Unfortunately, after years of patient study, circumstances over which Dr. Mera had no control delayed the publication of this monograph for twenty-five years. In the interim there have been constant inquiries for a reference work on Rio Grande blankets, indicating sustained public interest in the subject. This book is still the pilot work on the material even if it was completed a generation ago. Any additional details and insights on the history of Rio Grande Spanish weaving that have accumulated since were primarily the result of Dr. Mera's enthusiasm in persuading others to follow in his footsteps.

E. Boyd
March 27, 1965

5

Preface

It has been a little more than forty years since the writer first began to speculate as to the origin and history of Spanish-American harness-loom work, at that time such textiles being lumped under the common term, Chimayo. During the ensuing years a great many people, from time to time, have been interviewed, as occasions promising some bits of information arose, in an effort to arrive at some sort of connected story. My sincere thanks to all those who so patiently and willingly bore the brunt of my questioning, too many to list here, even if some miracle of memory should make it possible to recall every individual who contributed some item of interest.

In addition, every available source in literature was sought out, unfortunately with more disappointments than knowledge gained. Written history appears to have been vastly more concerned with political situations than with economic conditions or with smaller matters that daily affected the lives of the people. Seemingly, domestic weaving was deemed so commonplace that almost next to nothing concerning the industry appears in the annals of the past. In the course of time, from what was at first only a heterogeneous accumulation of informative items, a tenuous outline began to take shape, bit by bit. With this as a basis, it remained to effect correlations between this outline and the development of various design styles and the use of certain weaving materials. For completion of this last step, literally hundreds of blankets had to be studied, as opportunity permitted, to eliminate as far as possible any discrepancies.

Besides this, because some have held the belief that Spanish-American weaving stemmed directly from Pueblo Indian sources, evidence has been introduced to refute such a claim. As a part of this rebuttal, it has been thought best to include something of the history of loomwork by both the Indians and the Spanish colonists in order to demonstrate the point more clearly.

When it finally became evident there was little chance of securing additional information, it was obviously imperative that only the best in illustrative material be chosen to supplement the necessarily scanty text. To this end, requests were made to several individuals and institutions where desirable examples were known. In every instance, a ready response followed. I am greatly indebted to Mr. John Gaw Meem, from whose outstanding collection* of blankets the largest number selected for illustration were taken. Others contributing their share toward making the illustrative section of the monograph fully representative are: Mrs. Francis I. Proctor; Mrs. H. P. Mera; Mrs. Miguel Sanchez; Mr. Mitchell Wilder, who arranged a loan from the Taylor Museum; and the Laboratory of Anthropology. My sincere thanks to all of these.

*Subsequently donated to the Spanish Colonial Arts Society as the H. P. Mera Collection.

Spanish-American Blanketry

Of the hand-woven textiles produced by the various peoples who have made their home in the Southwest during the historic era, those of the Spanish colonists and their descendants have perhaps received as little attention as any. It is the aim of this monograph to correct this situation as far as possible, with an especial emphasis on their blanketry. Blankets woven by these relatively late-comers into Southwestern territory have been variously called Rio Grande, and Chimayo.[1]

The latter of these two terms is particularly objectionable, because of having too limited a connotation. Such usage tends to imply that the manufacture of all blankets of this general type had been carried on exclusively at the village of Chimayo. This estimate of the situation is far from the truth, for in reality, the weaving of textiles, being largely a home industry, is known to have been carried on at some time or other during each of the Spanish, Mexican, and American occupations of the area. Not only this, but the art appears to have been widespread, having been practiced to some extent in a great majority of the settlements lying along the course of the Rio Grande and its tributaries, in what is now New Mexico and southern Colorado.

There appear to be two main reasons why the name Chimayo, when referring to Spanish-American blanketry, has come into such extensive use. One reason for this may be that loom-work has been more or less continuous at that village, to a larger extent and perhaps for a greater length of time than elsewhere. This statement provides for the inclusion of the modern blankets, of a different type that are frequently observed in many present-day curio shops, a particular type

---

[1]Derived from Tsimajo, a Tewa Indian place name signifying "flaking stone of superior quality." J. P. Harrington, *The Ethnogeography of the Tewa Indians*, Bureau of American Ethnology, 29th Annual Report, p. 341. Washington, 1916.

largely developed in and about that settlement. Another reason seems to stem from a number of questionable statements published during the first part of the twentieth century. A sampling, typical of much that has been heretofore written on the subject, occurs in J. P. Harrington's paper, *The Ethnogeography Of The Tewa Indians,*[2] a study dealing particularly with a section of New Mexico once claimed by this linguistically related Indian group as their homeland, and in which the little community of Chimayo is located.

Harrington, in discussing the Indian name from which the Spanish word Chimayo is derived, first states: "The Indians say that Chimayo used to be a Tewa Indian pueblo, then called *Tsimajó onwi* (*onwi* = 'pueblo'). This pueblo was situated where the church now is, the informant stated." Following this, he cites a statement attributed to Edgar L. Hewett: " 'Chimayo was originally an Indian pueblo of blanket weavers.' " Harrington next quotes from an article in the *American Museum Journal:*[3] "Chimayo blankets made by Chimayo Indians of northern New Mexico, who are now practically extinct, are thought to be the connecting link between Navajo and Saltillo weaving." No author's name appears in connection with the article from which this quotation was taken. In the end, Harrington comes to the conclusion: "It is probable that the Chimayo blankets are a development of ancient weaving. No blankets are now woven by Tewa Indians, this art probably having been lost since the Mexicanization of the Tewa country. It is said that Chimayo blankets are woven also by Mexicans living at Sanctuario [a local name for that part of Chimayo lying south of the Santa Cruz river] and other places in the vicinity."

The appearance of pronouncements of this sort in publications of recognized scientific standing would naturally be accepted without question. In consequence the popular name, Chimayo blanket, can be laid to some such source.

Because in late years it has become increasingly apparent that many investigators of the early twentieth century were accustomed to accept as entirely credible, with few if any reservations, all information obtained from Indians, the writer decided to check the validity of statements regarding the former existence of a pueblo at, or closely adjacent to, the present village of Chimayo. A thorough and extended search of the locality revealed no traces of occupational debris such as is always present at former pueblo sites, anywhere about the church, near which the settlement was said to have been located. The sole

---

[2]Bureau of American Ethnology, 29th Annual Report, pp. 341–342. Washington, 1916.
[3]Vol. XII, No. 1, p. 33. 1912.

sign of anything suggestive of pre-Spanish occupation in that general vicinity was furnished by a handful of potsherds picked up on a small knoll a considerable distance to the north and near the eastern limit of the village proper. The sherds were all of a type of pottery known by archaeologists to be of twelfth century age, far too early to account for the transmittal of a weaving technique by any local Indian group to the Spanish colonists, who did not arrive on the site until more than 400 years later.

Other evidence tending to confirm the view that no prior Indian settlement had existed at this precise place late enough to have come in contact with the white invaders is contained in a document attributed to the reconqueror, de Vargas. It bears a date of 1695. A translation is given in *The Leading Facts of New Mexico History*.[4] In this, de Vargas assures the settlers of their continued rights to holdings in Chimayo, which they had had to abandon at the time of the Pueblo uprising of 1680, thus implying that that village had previously been Spanish rather than Indian. There is also included in the same reference a reply to a protest lodged by these petitioners to a proposed settlement of some Tano Indians from the Pueblo of San Cristóbal, whose original homes farther to the south had become untenable due to continual raids by the Apache. The objection was overruled, but because of a number of discouraging factors, including marked hostility on the part of the Spanish colonists, the newcomers remained but a short time. So short, in fact, that it seems, under the circumstances, improbable that any textile art could have been taken over from this harassed group. The site of this occupation has been definitely located a few miles west of the actual location of Chimayo. Finally, it may be pointed out that the name Chimayo does not occur in any documented reference to aboriginal pueblos.

In the face of all this, it would seem better to discount all former fanciful and unsubstantiated tales regarding a continuity of weaving from Indian to white man in a mythical Indian pueblo at Chimayo. Hence, the term Chimayo blanket should be restricted to those particular styles originating in and about that village, sometime about the close of the nineteenth and the beginning of the twentieth centuries. Because of such restriction, it then follows that the more inclusive name, Rio Grande blanket, should be preferred when speaking in a general way of all the blanketry woven by the Spanish colonists and their successors in the craft whose early settlements lay largely within the drainage of the stream bearing that name.

---

[4] R. E. Twitchell, Vol. III, p. 509. Torch Press, Cedar Rapids, Iowa, 1917.

There remains another and more cogent reason for doubting that any borrowing took place. This is contained in the fact that all true Rio Grande blankets can, with no particular difficulty, be shown to have been woven on horizontal harness looms of presumably European derivation, as distinct from the primitive upright sort used by the Indians. This technique represents the continuation of a custom of more than thirteen centuries duration. So different are the methods of operating these two forms of loom that there appears to be slight chance of any direct derivation in times past of one from the other.

Because the harness-loom technique, as it closely follows European procedure, must be regarded as intrusive in the Southwest, it will be a matter of some interest to determine, if possible, at least approximately the time of its introduction. In order to attempt anything of this nature it will be necessary to cite and to comment on the few available items to be found in the literature relating to the craft as a whole.

In order to present a clearer picture of the relationship of the two forms of loom-work, something of the status of aboriginal weaving in the Southwest during the first years of the Spanish conquest will be abstracted from observations made by a number of the early chroniclers.

The earliest mention of the art is contained in an account of the Coronado expedition of 1540, the first to explore this previously unknown region. In Winship's translation of the Castañeda narrative,[5] it is learned that in what he called the province of Tiguex, there were situated twelve villages, in which men did the spinning and weaving. Another reference from the same source describes the demand and seizure by the intruders of three hundred or more woven "cloaks of cloth" from the inhabitants, in order to augment a dwindling supply of clothing. Finally, in this same document the weaving of cotton blankets is also noted for the people of the Cíbola villages, the descendants of whom are now known as the Zuñi. Following the ill-fated Coronado party's withdrawal from the region, the Indians were left undisturbed for a little more than forty years.

The next incursion by Europeans in force took place in the year 1581, when Rodriguez and his followers made their way into Pueblo territory. Hernan Gallegos, the chronicler of this *entrada*, speaks of cotton garments being worn by the native inhabitants. This expedition, in turn, found it necessary to withdraw from the country after a limited sojourn. The following year witnessed the

---

[5]Bureau of American Ethnology, 14th Annual Report, Part 1, pp. 495, 521. 1895.

12

arrival of Espejo's band of explorers. In Luxan's journal, which records the events taking place during this latter venture, figures are cited that give some idea of the extent to which weaving was practiced among the Pueblo peoples of those times. A number of excerpts dealing with this matter are here quoted from Hammond and Rey's translation of that interesting document.[6]

During an account of the expedition's tour of the Hopi villages, the manner of reception accorded the strangers is discussed. Regarding a visit to "Aguato" (Awatovi), he states: "and they offered in all, together six hundred widths of blankets small and large, white and painted, so that it was a pleasant sight to behold." At "Gaspe" (Walpi), "Then they brought six hundred pieces of painted and white blankets and small pieces of their garments." The loot from two other pueblos, "Comupaui" (Shongopovi), and "Majanani" (Mishongnovi), taken together, is enumerated: "Then they brought about six hundred large and small pieces of blankets." Lastly, at "Olalla" (Oraibi), it is learned that: "They presented us with over eight hundred pieces of blankets, large and small, much spun and raw cotton." All this would amount to some twenty-six hundred garments. Although such figures may have been exaggerations, it is apparent from this and previous references, that a knowledge of weaving was generally widespread among all the sedentary Pueblo-dwelling peoples and that considerable amounts of cloth were being produced prior to the appearance of the Spanish invaders.

Before proceeding further it will be well to explain that the English terms "blanket" and "cloak," which appear in most of the translations previously quoted, normally apply to an article of attire, best expressed in Spanish by the word *manta*. This traditional form of Indian garment is of an oblong, rectangular shape and serves as a wrap-around dress, which can also be draped over the shoulders as a shawl. As will be seen, the name occurs frequently in many of the later records, shortly to be brought to attention.

The familiarity of the Indians with a successful weaving technique, on a loom of their own devising, was by no means overlooked by the Spanish colonists, the first of whom arrived with the Oñate expedition in 1598. That the newcomers quickly availed themselves of this knowledge is made abundantly plain in documents dating after that time. This eventually led to a degree of exploitation and oppression that ended in virtual serfdom for the aborigines, a condition which

---

[6]Quivira Society, Vol. 1, pp. 98, 100-102. 1929.

saw little relaxation for well over a century. A number of citations will be given which in themselves, and with their implications, will amply corroborate such a statement.

An additional factor becomes intrusive into the weaving situation sometime during the first half of the colonial period. This has to do with the introduction of wool as a medium for weaving, numbers of sheep having been brought in by the immigrants. Before the arrival of these animals, cotton and other vegetal substances were the materials employed in the textile industry; but from the evidence, it does not appear to have been overly long before the Indians became accustomed to deal successfully with the new fiber. There is a strong probability that this was due to an insistence on the part of the colonists, as woolen goods would more closely follow Spanish usage.

A supplementary item, which may be of interest to insert here, as it reflects something of the importance of Indian weaving, is in regard to the status assumed in the economy of the colony by the garment known to them as the *manta*. It will be recalled that the first mention of this article of apparel was in 1540, and it occurs in connection with a requisition or seizure during the Coronado campaign, purely as a matter of necessity. It appears possible that knowledge of this or of similar events eventually became broadcast throughout the entire Pueblo domain, and in consequence the appeasement of the conquerors with gifts of clothing came to be deemed a diplomatic measure.

This view could account for the large amounts of woven materials said to have been presented to the Spanish by the Hopi villagers, as mentioned above. In the long run, such a course of behavior seems to have ended in establishing some sort of pattern, for it will be seen that during the period of settlement and for some time afterward, the *manta* came to be regarded almost as a form of legal tender for the payment of assessments, fines, etc. This is clearly shown in the two following references taken from F. V. Scholes' "Church and State in New Mexico."[7] Speaking of a payment of tribute due in 1613 from the Pueblo of Taos, this item occurs: "The *mantas* are now ready and the governor should send for them."

Again, about this same time, an effort was being made by the authorities to correct some of the abuses against the Indians. In speaking of this, Scholes says: "To keep the peace and set some limits to the actions of irresponsible citizens,

---

[7]*New Mexico Historical Review*, Vol. XI, No. 1, pp. 33, 48. 1936.

Peralta (then Governor of the province) had issued decrees imposing damages in the form of *mantas* and a penalty of ten days imprisonment for offenses against the Indians. On one *encomendero* [a person officially licensed to make use of a system of enforced labor], Peralta imposed a fine of fifty *mantas* and fifty *fanegas* [Spanish bushels] of maize for various offenses. Seeing that the governor actually executed the decrees, the Indians, 'greedy for mantas,' provoked and incited the Spaniards to commit acts of violence in order to claim damages.'' Quoting further from Scholes' paper[8] regarding conditions existing during the governorship of de Baeza, (1634-37): "In all the Pueblos the Indians were forced to weave and paint great quantities of *mantas*, buntings and hangings, and some of the pueblos that did not raise enough cotton 'to cover their own nakedness' were obliged to barter with other villages for the cotton needed." The reference here to painting quantities of *mantas*, buntings, and hangings, incidently, concerns a now obsolete type of textile decoration. The exact nature of the method employed has been lost, no known examples showing such a treatment having survived to the present. Fabrics of this character, however, were called to attention by Spanish explorers as early as 1581.

Another item illustrating to what extent the Indians were compelled to weave for their masters is contained in L. B. Bloom's *A Trade Invoice of 1638*.[9] This citation has an added importance because, so far as the writer has been able to determine, it includes by inference the first mention of the use of wool for textiles. Omitting all but the woven goods comprised in an itemized shipment sent by Governor Luis Rosas to Mexico for sale, the following list is given:

Nineteen pieces of *sayal* [a coarse woolen cloth used as cheap dress goods] containing 1,900 *varas* [a unit of measurement equaling about 33 inches]
also; a box No. 1, containing 12 hangings
also; another No. 2, with 11 hangings
also; another No. 3, with 13 hangings
also; another No. 4, with 63 small blankets *(mantas)*
also; another No. 5, with 63 small blankets and 6 drapes *(antepuertas)*
also; another No. 6, with 13 hangings
also; another No. 7, with 68 blankets
also; another No. 8, with 68 blankets
also; another No. 9, with 33 drapes
also; another No. 10, with 30 blankets
also; another No. 11, with 60 blankets
also; another No. 13, with 64 blankets
also; another No. 14, with 11 hangings
also; No. 15, with 7 drapes, 8 underskirts *(faldellines)*, 19 large doublets and 2 small ones.

[8]*New Mexico Historical Review*, Vol. XI, No. 3, p. 287. 1936.
[9]*New Mexico Historical Review*, Vol X, No. 3, pp. 242–248. 1935.

Commenting on this, Bloom says: "It would be interesting, for example, to know by whom, and under what conditions, nineteen pieces of *sayal,* each a hundred *varas* in length, were produced. Possibly the wool was prepared and the weaving done in the various pueblos, but more probably an *obraje,* or workshop, was operated in Santa Fe with weavers secured from the pueblos under the *encomienda* system."

One other seventeenth century reference occurs in another paper by Bloom, *Early Weaving in New Mexico.*[10] In this is given an abstract from an edict issued by Governor Peñalosa Brizeno in 1664 which forbade "the masters of doctrine to employ Indian women in spinning, weaving *mantas,* stockings, or any other things without express license from me or him who may govern in my place."

From the preceding references it appears more than probable that most, if not all, of the fabrics used by the settlers were the product of enforced Indian labor, a condition which probably prevailed until the expulsion of the Spaniards at the time of the Pueblo rebellion in 1680.

With regard to the sort of loom employed during this period, it would appear that due to the efficiency of the native weavers in the use of their own type of weaving device, there would have been no particular necessity for an introduction of the European harness loom, although such a possibility cannot be entirely ruled out.

Following the rebellion, the Indians earned a respite of twelve years duration, unmolested by the Spanish. In 1692, the country was again subjugated by a military force under de Vargas. Shortly thereafter, the colonists returned and reoccupied the lands that they had been forced to abandon.

During most of this second and final period of white occupation, while it is known that enslavement of the Indians did not entirely cease, it also becomes evident that the day of wholesale exploitation was largely over, particularly if the records concerning weaving may be taken as an index. The Pueblo craftsman apparently ceased to occupy a prominent place in the colonial scheme. In fact, references to the craft as a whole in the eighteenth century are fewer than one might be led to expect, judging from the conditions prevailing during the previous century.

The earliest of these references, surprisingly, occurs in a report on the Navajo by Sergeant Major Don Joachin Codallos y Rabal, wherein are reported depositions taken from twelve men who had previously entered the country occupied

---

[10]*Ibid.*

16

by those people at various times ranging from 1706 to 1743. All witnesses agreed that at the time of their several visits the weaving of woolen textiles was definitely being carried on. The first mentioned date is so far the earliest documented record of weaving by any tribal group outside of what was normally Pueblo territory. Whether the weaving was being done by the Navajo themselves or by Pueblo refugees who had joined them during the years following the rebellion, in order to escape the wrath of the returning Spanish, is not made clear. It must, however, be presumed that it was from these fugitives that the Navajo acquired their knowledge of weaving on the indigenous vertical loom, a form which they have never since discarded. A translation and discussion of the Rabal manuscript will be found in *Some Navajo Cultural Changes During Two Centuries.*[11]

Following in chronological sequence, though very much later, we get a brief glimpse of the status of weaving throughout the colony in 1777 in a complaint made by Governor Mendinueta[12] concerning export of sheep and wool. Although unfortunately no hint is given as to whether white or Indian artisans were meant, the Governor said: "From the lack of the latter [sheep] results the lack also of mutton and wool, because by exporting of this species both in sheep and uncarded wool, the looms on which it is being utilized are idle." This is the earliest reference that may be logically construed to mean the manufacture of textiles by the colonists. After that year, all available citations up to the end of the eighteenth century deal principally with Navajo weaving. In spite of the stress laid on Navajo production, and although no mention occurs in governmental accounts, there is good evidence, to be cited a little later, to show that the harness loom had in reality finally arrived on the scene, at least by the middle of the eighteenth century, though the output from this source must have been deemed too small to deserve much official mention. It seems probable that by this time importations of commercially manufactured textiles through Mexico and those obtained by trade with the Navajo were sufficient to supply the greater share of the settlers' needs.

Next in chronological order is a reference supplied by C. A. Amsden in a paper entitled "Navajo Origins."[13] In this he quotes from a letter written in 1780 by Teodoro de Croix, Commander-General of the Interior Provinces of New Spain, to

[11]W. W. Hill, *Essays in Historical Anthropology of North America*, Smithsonian Miscellaneous Collections, Vol. 100, pp. 395-415. 1940.
[12]L. B. Bloom, "Early Weaving in New Mexico." *New Mexico Historical Review*, Vol. II, No. 3, p. 230. 1927.
[13]C. A. Amsden, *New Mexico Historical Review*, Vol. VII, No. 3, p. 204. 1932.

his superior, José Gálvez.[14] Here it is stated that: "The Navajos, who, although of Apache kinship, have a fixed home, sow, raise herds, and weave their blankets and clothes of wool."

For the year 1791, Bloom[15] has this to say: "There is reference in Governor de la Concha's correspondence to his having initiated trade by the Navajos in the exporting of pelts and coarse blankets." Another item abstracted from the same paper bears a somewhat later date, 1795. This was taken from a letter written by Fernando de Chacón, then Governor, to the *commandante* in Chihuahua, Mexico, and reads as follows in regard to the Navajo: "They work their wool with more delicacy and taste than the Spaniards." Concerning the situation in 1799, Amsden[16] furnishes an additional and interesting piece of information. He states in part in his "Navajo Origins": "Don José Cortez, 'an officer of the Spanish royal engineers, when stationed in that region,' wrote then that 'the Navajos have manufactures of serge, blankets, and other coarse cloths, which more than suffice for the consumption of their own people; and they go to the province of New Mexico with the surplus, and there exchange their goods for such others as they have not, or for implements they need.' "

It is plain, from remarks occurring in the documents of the latter part of the eighteenth century, that the Spanish authorities in the colony were becoming concerned with the unsatisfactory state of domestic weaving in the various settlements. In 1803, Salcedo, in Chihuahua, transmitted a royal order to Governor de Chacón which directed him to report on the state of agriculture, industry, the arts, and trade in his territory. Replying in the same year, Chacón seems to have attempted to put the best possible face on what must have been a rather indifferent situation. Again quoting from Bloom[17]: "With respect to arts and trades, it may be said with propriety that there are none in this Province, there being no apprenticeship, official examination for master-workmen, any formality of trade-unions, or other things customary in all parts, but necessity and the natural industry of these inhabitants has led them to exercise some, for example weaving in wool, shoemaker, carpenter, tailor, blacksmith, and mason in which nearly all are skilled." The weavers in wool, working on narrow racks, produced "narrow *bayetones* (baize), long *fresadas* (kind of blanket), *serapes, bayetas, sayal* (sackcloth), and *gergo* (carpeting), which weaves the y color with indigo *(añil)*

---

[14]Translation by A. B. Thomas, *Forgotten Frontiers*, p. 144. 1932.
[15]L. B. Bloom, *New Mexico Historical Review*, Vol. II, No. 3, p. 232. 1927.
[16]C. A. Amsden, *New Mexico Historical Review*, Vol. VII, No. 3, p. 206. 1932.
[17]L. B. Bloom, *New Mexico Historical Review*, Vol. II, No. 3, pp. 233–234. 1927.

and Brazil nut which they import from the outer country, and with stains and herbs which they know. From cotton they make a kind of domestic shirting *(manta)* of twisted thread closer and stronger than that of Puebla [the Mexican city], cloths for tablecloths, and stockings; and altho by the present Government said workmen in wool have been furnished with models of fulling-mill and press, they have not been able to make use of one or the other machine, on pretext of not being able to meet the expense." As will later be seen, this report eventually resulted in instructors in weaving being sent from Mexico, who conducted a school where the art was taught for a number of years.

Returning once more to the subject of Pueblo Indian weaving, it is rather surprising that not a single reference seems to be available for any fabrics woven by these people during the entire eighteenth century, nothing but the products of the Navajo being mentioned. It is the more strange because of the extraordinary quantities of textiles accredited to these people during the previous century. If fabrics woven by the Pueblos in the years following the reconquest had held a place of even nominal economic importance, it seems hardly possible that more specific mention would not have been made in contemporary documents. Hence a progressively sharp falling off of loom-work among the Pueblos may be postulated in the years after 1700. The reason for this is at present obscure.

That such a decline did take place is verified in a report made in 1808 by Fray Josef Benito Pereyro of the Santa Clara Mission,[18] from which the following is abstracted: "The Indians have no other industries besides planting, except those of Laguna, Acoma, and Zuñi, who, in addition to this and the hunting of buffaloes and deer, which all pursue, occupy themselves in weaving *mantas* (blankets), *cottones* (cotton cloth), and *Tilmas* (shawls), to clothe themselves and trade with the settlers and Indians of other pueblos." It will be noticed that the Hopi villages were not included in Pereyro's report, where weaving has always held an important position. This omission was probably due to the missions in those pueblos being inactive at the time.

It is obvious from the above reference that weaving in all but the westernmost Pueblo towns had, apparently soon after the opening years of the eighteenth century, virtually been discontinued. In consequence, Pueblo weaving would seem to have no direct relationship with the development of the Rio Grande blanket, which, as far as any evidence goes, did not appear on the scene until about

---

[18]Census of the population of New Mexico and a report of each mission. *New Mexico Archives*, No. 1191.

the middle of that same century, well to the east of those villages where the art had still survived to some extent. This conclusion provides the principal excuse for so closely following what is known concerning the course of aboriginal weaving, and it should furnish food for thought for those professing to see a direct derivation of colonial loom-work from a Puebloan source.

In an endeavor to add to the scant references bearing on Spanish colonial weaving, the writer has made a study of a large number of recorded wills and other papers filed during the eighteenth century.[19] These, while instructive in many ways, cannot be said to add a great deal to the picture beyond tending to support the view that domestic loom-work held a place of no great economic importance in the colonies before the 1800s. Probably only enough goods were produced to supplement importations. However, one important matter was cleared up: namely, that harness looms were actually present in the colony by the middle of the eighteenth century. This type of loom is suggested by the kinds of accompanying accessories that were inventoried with them.

These testaments, in nearly every instance, were found to be minutely itemized, down to such unimportant details as a few bullets or even a single needle. Outside of livestock, the average list of chattels was usually greatly restricted, even by the most modest standards, both in number and variety. Under these conditions, it seemed probable that some idea regarding the status of weaving could be obtained from the listed number of items connected with the craft.

The earliest mention of any objects having directly to do with weaving in the colony occurs in a will of 1750. In the years following, references become somewhat more frequent, especially toward the opening of the nineteenth century, but not to an extent that would indicate anything like a going industry. There were in all only fourteen looms listed for the fifty-year period prior to 1800, of which one was described as old, another incomplete. A group of five possibly may represent a weaving establishment, or, quite as likely, were part of a merchant's stock in trade, judging from the character and quantity of the other articles itemized. The latter estate also declared six spinning wheels, and an equal number of these implements also accompany single looms in as many different bequests. In addition to the fourteen complete looms, a "weaving frame" and a "loom frame" are inventoried. Besides the wool cards, combs, and other accessories used in the process of spinning and weaving which occur in the same lists

_____

[19]Translations of the Spanish Archives of New Mexico.

20

with looms, there are, from time to time, a number of these objects listed independently of any kind of weaving device.

References to coloring matter which could be construed as possibly useful for dyeing purposes are few: a "red coloring" occurs but once, "four packages of vermillion" once, and an undifferentiated blue substance is twice listed. On the other hand, on three occasions a definite dyestuff is referred to, namely "campeche log wood," "a log of campeche wood," and "a campeche log," all practically synonomous terms. This was the familiar logwood dye used in the days before commercial sorts were readily available, and the color it produced may still be seen in occasional survivals of some of the older and more simply designed Rio Grande blankets. No mention has been found of the "Brazil nut" dye spoken of in the context of a previously cited document of 1803. It may be that brazilwood was intended, another well-known dye substance.

As the primary concern of this paper is with blanketry, all references to such articles were carefully noted in going over the various wills. Those found can be divided into several categories, but the class to which by far the greatest number of blankets were referable was that designated simply as "coarse." Another category was "campeche," a term undoubtedly indicating that some portions of these blankets had been colored with logwood dye. Several others were called "Villa Alta," possibly after a center of weaving in the State of Oaxaca, Mexico. Additional terms included "Indian" (Navajo); "Castilla," at present unidentifiable; and "figured," "camp," and "patio," the first of these being, of course, of indefinite provenience and the latter two possibly representing only another name for some of the coarse local weaves. Mention of the well-known Saltillo sarape does not occur during the eighteenth century and only once in a later testament dated 1839.

Another item often appearing in bequests, although at the moment seeming to bear little relationship to the subject in hand, has to do with the transference of certain Indian servants or slaves, at times qualified as Apache,[20] which were found listed with the other chattels. Later on, when the matter of Rio Grande blanket design is taken up, it will become apparent that some of these unfortunates in the end exerted a noticeable influence.

From all this it appears that harness looms were a comparatively scarce article in the colonies, even allowing that some owners may have disposed of a few

---

[20]"Apache de Navahu," or Navajo.

without the formality of a will or other instrument. Taking everything into consideration, harness-loom weaving appears to have undergone little, if any, advancement since its inception, probably near the middle of the eighteenth century, as far as any records show. As before noted, such a condition was the cause of some concern to the authorities, who took steps as early as 1803 to rectify the situation. Without going into the series of negotiations toward accomplishing such an end, it is learned that finally a contract was awarded to one "Don Ygnacio Ricardo Bazan, a certified master of weavers, and his brother Don Juan Bazan, tradesman of the same guild, to teach their art to the youths there."[21] These men arrived in Santa Fe from Mexico on March 3, 1807, and were still in New Mexico in 1814.

Thus for the first time, the services of expert professional craftsmen became available to the colonists. This move on the part of the authorities, according to the records, resulted in a marked improvement in technique. These same instructors were also quite probably responsible for the introduction of new concepts in design. It follows that although the coarsely woven and simply designed blankets of the 1700s may properly be considered as the earliest form of the Rio Grande blanket, it was due to the influence exerted by these teachers that what was once a merely utilitarian type of textile in time became one possessing a recognized esthetic value as well.

Up to this point, attention has been directed almost entirely to the various historical implications pertaining to the subject. Now the distinguishing characteristics of Spanish-American blanketry will be taken up. As an aid in that direction, certain comparisons will have to be made from time to time with the better known Navajo product, a type of blanket with which colonial work has sometimes been confused.

The weave can be defined as a simple tapestry, the warp elements being entirely concealed by those of the weft. This technique in the fabrication of blankets is a basic procedure in the Southwest, not only for the type under discussion but for those of the Navajo and Pueblo Indians as well. But unlike the two latter craftsmen, the colonial blanket weaver seems never to have attempted any sort of twilling.[22] Examples of this variant are seen only in the fabrics of contemporaneous aboriginal manufacture. Also, the use of rolled cloth strips[23] as a

[21]L. B. Bloom, *New Mexico Historical Review*, Vol. II, No. 3, p. 235.
[22]H. P. Mera, "Navajo Twilled Weaving," *Navajo Textile Arts*, p. 63. 1947.
[23]H. P. Mera, "Cloth-strip Blankets of the Navajo," *Navajo Textile Arts*, p. 69. 1947.

substitute for the woolen yarn normally employed—an occasional practice of the Navajo—has as yet been found in but a single example of the Rio Grande type, among the hundreds canvassed.

The definitive differences between blankets made by Indians and those of Spanish-American weavers are certain details of procedure incidental to the kind of loom used, whether woven on the primitive upright sort or the more mechanized form used by the latter group. Some of these details are of the utmost value in differentiating one kind from the other.

The old colonial harness loom was inclined to be rather narrow. It was usually only able to accommodate a width of textile not to exceed twenty-four inches, and many examples several inches under this measurement are known from looms of this type. For this reason, when a blanket was desired, two separate lengthwise strips were generally woven and then sewed together. There was one alternative, which called for a display of considerable ingenuity on the part of the weavers. On information furnished by several old-time weavers, we learn that this was accomplished by a method of stringing the loom with two sets of warp elements, one above the other. The weft was then carried, as in ordinary tapestry weaving, from one edge across the upper set of warps, brought down to the lower set, and continued for its full width in the opposite direction. The process was then reversed, first returning back to the edge where weaving was started. This procedure was repeated until a blanket of the desired length was obtained. Hence, when a single-piece Rio Grande blanket was found with the central warps doubled and spaced noticeably more closely together than any of the rest, it is good evidence that it had been woven in a manner similar to the one just described.

The principal advantage gained in resorting to this comparatively awkward method was that a bilateral symmetry of pattern could be easily maintained. On the other hand, when the two halves of a blanket had to be woven separately, it was difficult to weave them so that there would be a perfect register between both sections of the design when sewed together. Again, in many instances where two-strip weaving was pursued, a correspondence in coloration between one section and the other was not always of the best. This was due for the most part to a variation in the shades of colors occurring in different dye lots. A few examples are known wherein certain parts of a design on one lateral half of a blanket were woven in an entirely different color from that used in the corresponding motif on the other half (Plate 12). The preparation of insufficient material of the proper color could account for such a condition.

A close scrutiny of the plates will show several narrow-loomed blankets in which discrepancies of this sort are discernible. In much later years, looms wide enough to weave full-width blankets came into use, a marked advance over the tedious procedure once practiced on the narrow form of loom.

Examples of the one-piece Rio Grande blanket are usually the kind that are so often mistaken for Navajo work. Fortunately, there are certain technical features, the absence or presence of which can be relied upon to make identification a certainty. The two of these most easily checked are whether there are braided selvage cords incorporated in the web along the edges of all four sides, and also whether "lazy lines" can be found. The presence of either or both definitely indicates Navajo technique. Neither of these features can be successfully achieved on the harness loom. For those unacquainted with the term "lazy lines," these appear as faint diagonal markings on an otherwise smoothly woven surface and are due to a method of weaving a blanket on the upright loom in a series of blocks or sections. These sloping lines mark the locations where the sections abut on one another.

In lieu of the Navajo's arrangement of braided selvage cords for reinforcement of the edges, the Spanish-American weaver merely doubled, trebled, or more rarely, quadrupled his outer warp elements to serve a similar purpose. No particular effort was expended to reinforce the ends, the excess lengths of warp being allowed to protrude beyond the web, where they were gathered into groups and knotted in various ways. Still another peculiarity distinguishing this type from others in the region is that each individual warp element was normally composed of two members twisted together, as opposed to a single, tightly spun strand preferred by the Indian weaver.

Two-strand warp was the rule until comparatively late times, especially when handspun yarns were used. However, in more recent years there has arisen some variation in this respect. In some late examples where common cotton twine had been selected for warp material, the elements were frequently not paired. Also after machine-spun woolen yarns became available through importation, these were likewise used not only for warp but for weft as well. When commercial yarn was chosen for warp, it has been observed that single strands were employed, probably because in these types each strand was already made up of several plies. Despite the fact that a variety of different materials, ranging from handspun to machine spun, entered into the weaving of the Rio Grande blanket during the course of its existence, the principal details of technique remained quite stable.

Although woolen yarns of one sort or another were customarily used for weft elements, there were, nevertheless, very rare occasions when other kinds of fiber were substituted. A notable exception to the rule is furnished by four blankets in which white handspun cotton was used for everything except the several decorative effects. In the composition of these designs, dyed wools were employed solely (Plate 13). Another aberrant specimen examined included some brown stripes woven from a yarn having a peculiarly puzzling appearance. This, upon analysis by competent authorities, proved to have been spun from the soft undercoat of the bison. The relative scarcity of such divergent examples can be judged when it is known that these few were the only ones occurring among the several hundred blankets inspected in the preparation of this study.

In contrast to a marked conservatism in regard to technical details, a great heterogeneity in design is manifest, instead of an orderly development along some specific line. It becomes evident, after studying a great deal of material, that at least two distinct sources were drawn upon for ideas on decoration. Some decorative schemes show direct derivation from one or the other, still others are plainly combinations of the two, while many seem to be referable to none in particular. This matter will receive further attention a little later in the discussion.

Curiously enough, almost a hundred years elapsed after the beginning of the nineteenth century before a cumulative blending of these diverse ideas crystallized into anything like a distinctive and more or less standardized style. This final phase is represented by the only type of blanket that may properly be called Chimayo, the kind most often to be seen by today's casual tourist (Plates 21 and 22).

Let us now go back to what appears to be the start of colonial blanket weaving in mid-eighteenth century. Judging from what little can be inferred from the scanty records of that time, when anything more elaborate than a plain, purely utilitarian type of article was wanted, various combinations of stripes furnished about the limit in decorative devices. This procedure was possible with the least technical skill. It seems likely that such a situation continued to prevail for a considerable time after the arrival of two instructors in weaving sent from Mexico in 1807. In substantiation of the view that no advance had been made over the simple arrangement of stripes, we must turn first to all the known examples of authentically dated Navajo blanketry of the early nineteenth century. This is necessary because there are no known examples of the early Rio Grande type that bear actual dates. Hence, a process of deduction must be relied upon. C. A. Amsden has illustrated examples of striped Navajo blanketry of this period in his comprehensive work, *Navajo Weaving*.[24] As the Spanish narrators of that general period consistently reported the superiority of Navajo blankets over those of the colonists, it seems reasonable to believe that such simple decorative schemes were then an accepted fashion for both groups. In support of the superiority of Navajo weaving, Don Pedro Pino in his *Exposición del Nuevo Mexico*, published in 1812, has this to say: "Their woolen fabrics are the most valuable in our province, and Sonora and Chihuahua." Plates 1, 2, and 3 illustrate examples of this early and comparatively simple type of Rio Grande blanket, wherein natural brown and white wools were used in color schemes in which indigo blue, logwood red-brown, chamiso yellow, and other shades derived from vegetal dyes had been used in combination.

Sometime between the arrival of the previously mentioned master weavers from Mexico in 1807 and the middle of the nineteenth century, a new style in Rio Grande blankets put in an appearance, exhibiting designs that were vastly more complex in structure than any of the previous weavings. The new style was obviously derived from some Mexican source, for the designs resembled in greater or lesser degree those typical of the more prominent blanket-weaving centers of that period, such as San Miguel de Allende and Saltillo, and perhaps others in the State of Oaxaca. Following a period of expert instruction by the teachers from Mexico, through whose services the ability to weave patterns of greater complexity was no doubt attained, it appears not unlikely that these men, because of a familiarity with the textiles of their own country, introduced the new style.

The principal reason for specifying a mid-nineteenth century date is that at least some blankets in the pseudo-Mexican style can be demonstrated to have been in production at that period. This should not be taken to mean that the style was not in existence for perhaps some time before. Our assumption regarding the dating of these blankets rests on the occasional inclusion of an easily identifiable imported three-ply yarn of European provenience. This same yarn occurs in dated Navajo work of the early 1860s, and it can be safely assumed that both kinds of blankets were woven at about the same time. In addition, an upper time limit for use of this so-called Saxony yarn can be postulated, because it does not seem to have been available in the Southwest much after the first half of the 1870s, having been largely superseded by four-ply domestic sorts then coming into use.

---

[24]Amsden's plates 61, 62, and 63.

Although some blankets in the Mexican-style group can be described as copies, a greater number appear to be merely adaptations, retaining many of the larger features of that general type of design but lacking a minuteness of detail and delicacy of treatment normally to be seen in the source material. Typical examples of this style are shown in Plates 4, 5, and 6. Before leaving the subject of the pseudo-Mexican blanket, it will be well to explain that this style in no way succeeded in doing away with the old striped design-formula, which persisted in the coarser weaves up to and somewhat beyond the beginning of the twentieth century.

While the foregoing development was proceeding in the Spanish-American weaving fraternity, a similar improvement was taking place in Navajo textiles. The peak of Navajo accomplishment was reached in the 1850s and 1860s, both in terms of technical excellence and design. Unlike the blankets of the Spanish-American, the "classic type of Navajo blanketry"[25] shows practically no trace of an outside influence.

Contrary to what might be expected in this particular period, there seems to have been no interchange of ideas on designing between the two schools of weaving. A little later, quite the opposite was true.

The finest type of pseudo-Mexican blanket became obsolescent by the late 1870s, and about that same time a hardly definable mixture of designs was coming into use, in which, for the most part, no one type can be said to have predominated. Features taken from the old striped forms were incorporated with others derived not only from Mexican sources but also from Navajo designs current at that time (Plates 7 to 14). In fact, so strong was the latter influence that examples are known where only the details of technique and coloration serve to distinguish them from Navajo work (Plates 15 and 16).

The question of just why Navajo ideas on decoration were so readily accepted at this stage but not at an earlier period cannot be answered. It seems strange, because the necessary contacts were not lacking at any time early in the eighteenth century. Not only were Navajo blankets a common article of trade in the settlements, but numbers of these same people were kept in a state of servitude by the settlers to perform domestic tasks and other forms of manual labor. According to all accounts, a great many of them were employed as weavers and became responsible for the curious fabrics known as "slave blankets."[26] These

---

[25]H. P. Mera, "Navajo Blankets of the 'Classic' Period," *Navajo Textile Arts*, p. 14. Laboratory of Anthropology, 1947.

[26]H. P. Mera, "The 'Slave Blanket', " *Navajo Textile Arts*, p. 21. Laboratory of Anthropology, 1947.

were woven on the aboriginal upright loom but display a curious blend of both Navajo and Rio Grande decorative styles and coloration, as well as some defection in regard to certain minor features of Navajo weaving technique.

The presence of these captives furnishes a plausible reason for Navajo influence in the period after 1870, but we cannot explain the lack of it a short time earlier, when equal opportunities for the exchange of ideas existed under what appear to have been exactly the same conditions. In turn, during this same period the Navajo can be shown to have borrowed certain units of design taken from Rio Grande blanket decoration and to have incorporated them with those of their own.

Eventually, out of such a hodge-podge of decorative concepts, there emerged something in the way of being distinctive, a type exhibiting a slight degree of specialization, sufficient perhaps to rank it as a distinct development. The outstanding feature of this type is an eight-pointed, star-like motif in the design, which though always present, varies in number and location on the field of decoration. Blankets of this class are locally known as Valleros, a name derived from the Spanish word *valle*, or in English, valley. This type is said to have once constituted a preferred style peculiar to some of the mountain valleys in southern Taos County, New Mexico. A commercial four-ply yarn, often spoken of as Germantown, was frequently employed in weaving the best examples. However, a single instance has come to attention wherein an earlier three-ply yarn was found to have been incorporated and a few others in which a fine grade of handspun material was employed. On rather scanty evidence, it is thought that the best examples of this style flourished for a limited time in the 1880s or slightly later. Finally, a greatly coarsened version appears to represent a survival of the style at a comparatively late date. Three Valleros blankets of the better sort are figured in Plates 17, 18, and 19.

Up to this point, attention has been focused mainly on the finer weaves—those having a distinctly esthetic appeal. However, some notice must also be given to a class in which coarsely spun yarns and an indifferent grade of loom-work were the rule rather than the exception. To neglect this phase of Rio Grande blanket weaving would most assuredly result in a very one-sided and incomplete account of the craft, as it is more than probable that the bulk of all Spanish-American blankets ever woven would be assignable to this category.

In keeping with inferior workmanship, all attempts at decoration were equally crude and were almost entirely confined to the use of simple bands or stripes in various harsh and garish colors, resulting from the use of aniline dyes. These coarsely woven, aniline-dyed forms first came into use in the Southwest late in the 1870s or early in the following decade. Such blankets are, technically and functionally, directly in a line of descent from those coarse utilitarian kinds first mentioned in the lists of bequests recorded in the eighteenth century. After that time, similar forms continued to be made in some of the rural sections, though in steadily diminishing numbers, until well into the first quarter of the twentieth century. Blankets of this character (Plate 20) were principally used in out-of-doors activities, where rough usage was to be expected; for example, as lap-robes, camp beds for herdsmen, and the like.

As the opening years of the twentieth century began to draw nearer, blanket weaving among the Spanish-speaking population appears to have become progressively of less and less importance, owing probably to the increasing ease with which commercially manufactured blankets could be obtained. Doubtless another factor contributing to this decline was the easy access to large quantities of the Navajo product which, from the first, had always offered serious competition.

It was about this time, when hand-weaving seemed on the point of nearly vanishing altogether, that a fortunate occurrence encouraged some weavers to return to their looms. This, however, affected only a comparatively small section of country in and about the little village of Chimayo. This localized revitalization of the craft came about through a demand on the part of certain dealers in curios in nearby Santa Fe for a moderately priced article for tourist consumption. From that time to the present great quantities of a distinctive type of textile have been produced, not only in the form of blankets, but also articles such as pillowtops and narrow runners. It is this class of loom-work alone that can consistently bear the name Chimayo.

Technically, the true Chimayo blanket tends to follow traditional procedure in all but a few minor details. It is woven in a single piece on a loom of corresponding width, without resort to some special method, as was earlier the case when the old narrow form of that apparatus appears to have been used exclusively. Another difference is seen in the make-up of the warp elements. In the new type of fabric, four-ply machine-spun wool yarn was used for these in place of the older form made up of single strands of handspun twisted in pairs. Not only does the warp consist of commercial material but a similar kind of yarn is also employed for the weft.

Turning to the subject of design, it is readily apparent that in Chimayo work this feature possesses a distinctive character all its own. Just why the principal units of decoration should differ so greatly from any of those preferred in the preceding periods cannot be satisfactorily determined at this time, the type having already been in existence for more than forty years. With exceedingly few exceptions, the decorative scheme of the Chimayo blanket employs one of those curiously conceived units, which normally occupies a prominent place in the center of the field. Some weavers are content to make this unit the sole attempt at decoration, while in other cases additional motifs of secondary importance are seen. There are also transverse bands and stripes of contrasting colors situated near either end. Two characteristic examples of the Chimayo type are pictured on Plates 21 and 22.

There can be little doubt that most, if not all, of the centrally located designs were distantly inspired by those similarly placed lozenge-shaped devices that are so characteristic of many Mexican and pseudo-Mexican blanket styles (Plate 4). For this reason, it might be expected that a series of transitional forms between the two could be found. However, little that is indicative of a gradual transition has yet been noted, though we see enough to make a direct relationship a logical deduction. Altogether it begins to look as if this peculiar style must have sprung almost fully developed from the mind of someone skilled in the adaptation of design, rather than having been the result of any orderly evolutionary process. It may be that the unknown designer, because of dealing with a purely commercial article, created a form of decoration in which elongate horizontal areas held a prominent place, thus assuring greater facility in weaving. This would tend to increase the output materially by a saving in time.

Thus it is seen that at one stage in the history of the Rio Grande blanket, Indian ideas on decoration threatened to exert a considerable influence. Today, the most prominent units of design in use are those derived, however remotely, from the classic period of Hispano-Mexican styling.

In connection with this latest development, there is another feature, or perhaps more accurately a phase, which in a sense might be classed as something in the way of a revival. This variation from typical Chimayo blanketry came about through the desire of a limited section of the buying public for a blanket in which some of the older and more conservative styles, both in design and coloring, could be reproduced at a cost much less than that of an antique specimen. To satisfy this demand, one of the Chimayo weavers, more than a decade ago, began to experiment. Eventually an article was produced that met most of the requirements.

Instead of the usual commercial Germantown yarn, with its somewhat harsh quality, a softer, though still machine-spun material, was substituted. With this exception, as far as technique goes, the new product is the same as the ordinary Chimayo blanket. Beyond the possession of a more pleasing texture, the most noticeable difference lies in the selection of colors and designs. These were copied or adapted from among the simplest and most dignified of the older styles, including the best in both striped and patterned sorts. Unfortunately, this attempt seems not to have met with enough popular approval to continue the effort, and few if any of this kind are now being woven. Plate 24 illustrates a typical example.

With the description of this latter variant, the history of Spanish-American blanketry in the southwestern United States is brought up to the present, insofar as documented records and oral information have been made available. At the moment, there seems to be little chance of further development along this particular line, since the type as it appears today has, for so many years, had a firmly established status as an object intended largely for sale by dealers in souvenirs and curios. That attempts to duplicate anything like the achievements of the past are apparently destined to prove unavailing is evidenced by a number of decisive failures to bring back handspun yarns and a true revival of the old styles (Plate 23). All the efforts to accomplish this have thus far come to naught. The failure is largely due to the cost of production under modern standards of compensation.

It may be of interest to call attention to one of the latest applications of hand-weaving on the colonial type harness loom, which, although unconnected with the subject of blanketry, still has to do with Spanish-American textile art. The reader may remember that in some of the documented accounts of loom-work pertaining to the early eighteenth century, several fabrics other than blankets were mentioned. Some of these were plainly intended for use in the making of clothing. But as time progressed, imported commercial cloths appear to have eventually displaced the locally woven kinds, and it is only recently that anything except the Chimayo type of article has been attempted. At the present, however, hand-woven piece-goods for dresses, neckties, and the like are once more being produced. This new trend in the industry bids fair to have a favorable economic future.

Plates

Plate 1
Early Striped Style

*A*lthough not accurately datable, this blanket typifies an early fashion in which decoration was confined to narrow stripes. Despite the lack of a specific date, a respectable age is suggested because of the use of handspun yarns colored with, to quote a document of 1803, some of the "stains and herbs they know." The several shades of yellow and green were obtained through the use of a dye extracted from a shrub called *chamiso*, a common and easily prepared coloring agent. The occasional blue stripes that have been introduced here and there were dyed with indigo, or *añil* as it was then known, an importation into the colonies, probably through Mexico.

Date: 1870s (?). Size: 82 by 51 inches. Two widths. Warps: 8 per inch; two-ply, Z-spun, S-twisted handspun wool; natural white, gray, and brown. Wefts: 28 per inch; one-ply Z-spun handspun wool; natural brown and white, indigo blue, vegetal gold (possibly walnut) and green.[1]

Spanish Colonial Arts Society, Inc. Collection on loan to the Museum of New Mexico at the Museum of International Folk Art. Gift of Mr. and Mrs. John Gaw Meem, H. P. Mera Collection. L.5.62.69.

---

[1]The portions of the figure captions presented in italic type are additions by Kate Peck Kent.—Ed.

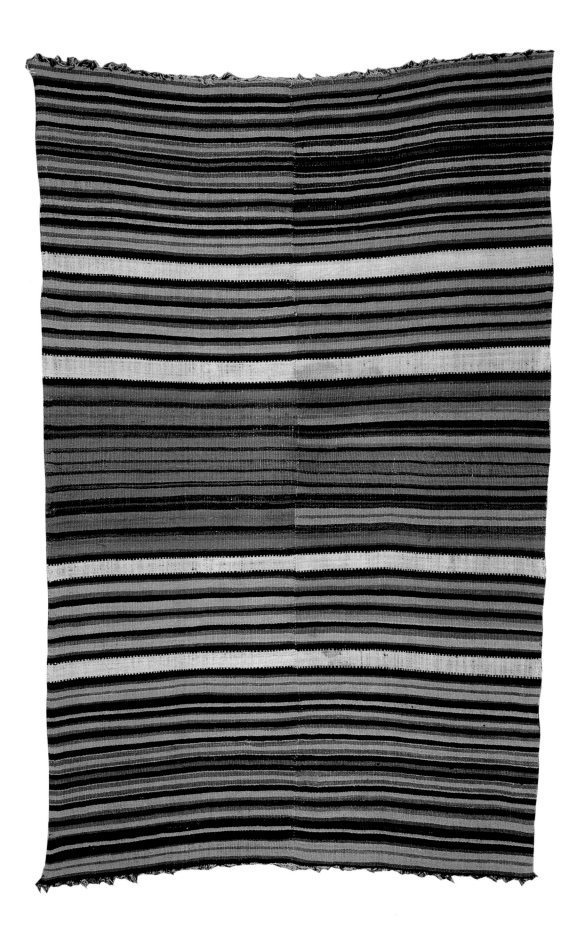

Plate 2
Early Striped Style

*A*nother example with decoration restricted to striping is shown here, particularly to illustrate the use of a dye that seems to have been greatly esteemed at least as early as the latter part of the eighteenth century. This coloring matter was obtained from logwood, or "Campeche wood" as it was sometimes called in documents of that period. Originally of a somewhat dullish crimson hue, with age and repeated visits to the tub, old textiles of this kind tend to fade to a pinkish brown or, in extreme cases, even to a light tan. Nevertheless, if the fibres of a section of old yarn be separated, traces of the original color can usually be detected deep in the interior. In addition to the dominant color, narrow stripes of indigo blue and *chamiso* yellow may be seen. Handspun yarn was employed throughout. Today this kind is familiarly called a "brazil." This usage may be accounted for by the fact that, although logwood and brazilwood may be botanically distinct, both yield haematoxylin dyes possessing practically the same properties. It is quite probable that both substances were used from time to time, more or less interchangeably; therefore, the present name may as well be retained because of long established usage.

Date: 1850s. Size: 92½ by 52 inches. One width, double woven. Warps: 6 per inch; two-ply, Z-spun, S-twisted handspun wool; natural white and gray-brown. Wefts: 36 per inch; one-ply, Z-spun handspun wool; natural white and brown, indigo blue, indigo and natural blue-green, and natural yellow and red-brown. The latter is not brazilwood or logwood but may be a red dye wood related to brazilwood. Dye analyzed by Saltzman.

Spanish Colonial Arts Society, Inc., Mera Collection, at MNM. L.5.62.70.

Plate 3
Early Striped Style

*B*lack and a blue serve to make up the entire color scheme in the present example. In this blanket and other ones, where stripes alone were used to achieve the decorative effect, especially when there were few color contrasts, any tendency toward monotony was met by varying the widths, spacing, and texture of the various components. The yarns used for the black areas, especially in the earlier weaves, were either dyed with a locally concocted dyestuff or were spun from the wool of the so-called black sheep, the latter being distinguished by a more brownish tinge. Finely woven handspun blankets of this general type, which adhere to the formula calling for stripes in indigo blue and black, appear to represent a very popular fashion in the past. This premise is made on the grounds that a large majority of all the appreciably older Rio Grande blankets are of this sort. Many collectors and dealers refer to these as "old blues."

Date: 1860s. Size: 102 by 51 inches. One width, double woven. Warps: 6 per inch. Wefts: 40 per inch; one-ply, Z-spun handspun wool; natural black and white and indigo blue.

School of American Research Collections in the Museum of New Mexico, Laboratory of Anthropology 9534/12.

Plate 4
Psuedo-Mexican Blanket

*J*o the casual observer, blankets belonging in this division may be thought, at first sight, to be of Mexican provenience. Such a view is quite excusable, because some of the larger features of design closely follow those of similar textile forms which are typical of that country. Two of the most prominent of these features are a lozenge-shaped or diamond-shaped device, or an adaptation of it, occupying the center of the field, and elaborately patterned lateral borders. However, a comparison with Mexican design will immediately demonstrate that the decorative units in the Rio Grande forms are coarser and more simply conceived than those of the alien article. Because of these broad similarities, the term pseudo-Mexican will be applied to this class of domestic textile. The style appears to have originated from the influence of Mexican instructors who were sent to the colonies to teach weaving in 1807.

This example was woven almost entirely of handspun yarn, the exception being the areas in red, for which a three-ply imported yarn was employed. This latter material is known to have been in use in the 1860s and on into about the first half of the following decade.

Date: about 1860. Size: 83½ by 49 inches. Two widths. Warps: 10 per inch; two-ply, Z-twisted, handspun wool, white. Wefts: 36 per inch; one-ply, Z-spun, handspun wool, natural white and black-brown, and indigo blue. Also three-ply, Z-spun, S-twisted commercial wool in pale orange and natural yellow; and the same type of yarn doubled, in cochineal red and natural yellow. Red dye analyzed by Saltzman.

Spanish Colonial Arts Society, Inc., Mera Collection, at MNM. L.5.62.85.

Plate 5
Pseudo-Mexican Blanket

*B*elonging in the same category as the blanket appearing in the preceding plate in regard to both color and design, this is an unusually ornate example of the pseudo-Mexican blanket. As in many others in the group, an elaboration of the usual diamond-shaped unit occupies a central position; also present are the conventional ornamental borders. Both features are distinguishing marks of the style. The background, or field, instead of containing the more characteristic small design elements, is taken up by a doubled series of adaptations of the lozenge motif. Here again, both handspun and three-ply yarns are included in the weft, thus postulating contemporaneity with the example just described.

Date: 1870. Size: 85 by 45½ inches. Two widths. Warps: 10 per inch; two-ply, Z-spun, S-twisted handspun wool, white. Wefts: 36 per inch; two-ply, S-spun, S-twisted handspun wool, white and red/white raveled, recarded, and respun. Also three-ply, Z-spun, S-twisted yarns, probably handspun, in an unknown mauve dye; and handspun yarns paired, in dark blue-green. Also commercial, three-ply, S-spun, Z-twisted yarn in chemical purple and turquoise dyes; and commercial, three-ply, Z-spun, S-twisted yarn in chemical dark red and unknown orange dye.

Although the yarns are rather heavy and the blanket feels like a Navajo piece of the 1880s, I would date it between 1870 and 1875 on the basis of the three-ply yarns and the recarded red/white. The dyes have not been tested.

Spanish Colonial Arts Society, Inc., Mera Collection, at MNM. L.5.62.83

Plate 6
Pseudo-Mexican Blanket

*T*his is a third and unique example of the Mexican type. Of particular interest is the field exhibiting a reticulated appearance. This results from converting fusiform units, such as those seen in Plate 8, into series of small, evenly and closely spaced diamonds. Such a placement is quite at variance with the treatment usually accorded such small units, which are normally widely distributed. The light-colored background showing between the darker diamond-shaped figures takes on the appearance of a white network.

The materials employed in weaving—handspun and three-ply yarns—are the same as those used in the two pseudo-Mexican blankets previously illustrated; therefore a like temporal position can be assumed.

Date: 1860. Size: 87½ by 48 inches. Two widths.

Private collection.

Plate 7
Hybrid Style

This example is a member of a comparatively loose grouping, wherein no single stylistic influence in design is consistently followed. Instead, traces of one or more extraneous influences may be seen in a single fabric, often in combination with original ideas of no particular derivation. For want of a more definitely descriptive title, this group will be included under the broadly inclusive heading of hybrid styles.

The blanket illustrated is a rather coarsely woven, handspun one. It makes use of a central diamond-shaped unit in indigo blue and black, derived from Mexican sources. So likewise is the field, with its sprinkling of dash-like elements, a not uncommon feature in old Saltillo sarape weaves. The stepped figures in the four corners, on the contrary, can be traced to no particular style and may be regarded as an expression of the weaver's personal fancy. Handspun yarn was used exclusively in weaving.

Date: before 1860. Size: 82 by 46½ inches. Two widths. Warps: 6 per inch; two-ply, Z-spun, S-twisted, handspun light and dark wool. Wefts: 28 per inch; one-ply, Z-spun, handspun wool; natural brownish black and white, and indigo dyed.

Spanish Colonial Arts Society, Inc., Mera Collection, at MNM. L.5.62.73.

Plate 8
Hybrid Style

*A*side from the small fusiform units scattered over three of the transverse bands into which this blanket is divided, there is little to show an affinity with anything but local styles. There may be a faint hint of the Navajo in the chevron-like arrangements occupying alternate bands, but nothing at all is definite. The first mentioned small units stand for the same idea as the dashes noted in the preceding description as a Saltillo derivative. Multiple stripes, of course, hark back to those normally present on Rio Grande blankets in an earlier day. Handspun yarn, dyed with commercial pigments, now pleasingly toned down by time, has been employed throughout.

Date: 1870s. Size: 82 by 44½ inches. Two widths. Warps: 7 per inch; two-ply, Z-spun, S-twisted, handspun wool, natural white. Wefts: 24 per inch; one-ply, Z-spun, coarse handspun wool; natural white and brown, and chemically dyed red, orange, green, yellow, magenta, and purple.

Spanish Colonial Arts Society, Inc., Mera Collection, at MNM. L.5.62.82.

Plate 9
Hybrid Style

*N*umerous short dashes and a lesser number of units having a somewhat hourglass shape constitute all the elements deemed necessary by the maker in designing the greater portion of this fabric. In the center of the field, the weaver has ingeniously arranged a group of the "hourglass" units into the semblance of a diamond-shaped device. It is quite obvious that this ornament, and the dashes as well, may be satisfactorily traced to Mexican influence, but the "hourglass" motifs cannot be positively identified with any other stylistic treatment. The yarn is all handspun. That of the red areas has been dyed with some sort of commercial dyestuff.

Many washings in waters of various temperatures and of varying mineral content sometimes end in distortions as shown here. This is due to uneven shrinkage which was greatly aided by variations in the quality of yarn.

Date: 1870s. Size: 80 by 42 inches. Two widths. Warps: 6 per inch; two-ply, Z-spun, S-twisted handspun wool, natural white. Wefts: 24 per inch; one-ply, Z-spun handspun wool, rather coarse and crimped; natural white, dark brown, and medium brown, and chemically dyed red.

Spanish Colonial Arts Society, Inc., Mera Collection, at MNM. L.5.62.75.

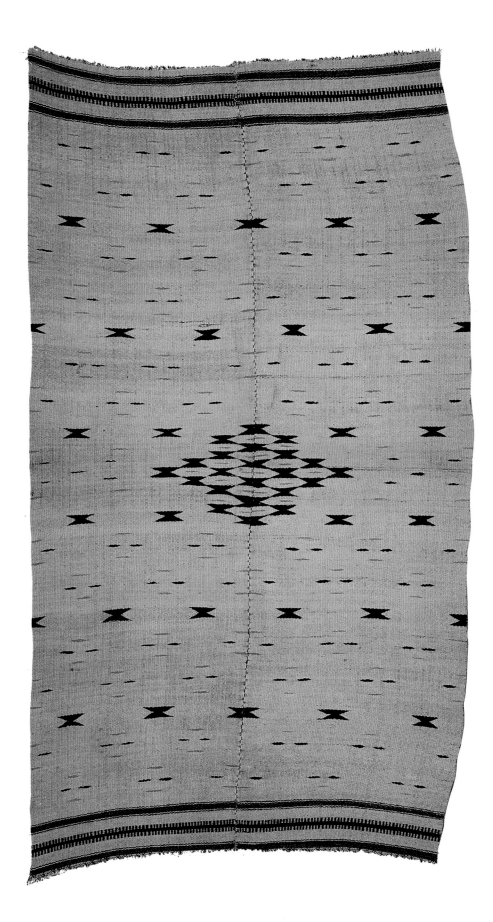

Plate 10
Hybrid Style

*I*n decided contrast to the three previously described specimens of the hybrid group of Rio Grande blankets, the example shown here has discarded the Mexican element, which is usually present to some extent, in favor of a Navajo-like concept. Although the design smacks strongly of Navajo styling, it falls short of much of the orderliness and accuracy of spacing that is typical of the work of the Indian craftsman. Such a lack is particularly noticeable in the bands of decoration next in order to the two endmost.

Added confirmation of its origin is evidenced by the fact that it was woven in two sections, with other technical details indicating the use of a harness loom. Besides handspun yarns of black and indigo blue, three-ply commercial material was employed for the colored sections. Because of this, the period of manufacture is placed sometime in the 1870s.

Date: 1870. Size: 85 by 52½ inches. Two widths. Warps: 6 per inch; two-ply, Z-spun, S-twisted handspun wool, white. Wefts: 32–33 per inch; one-ply, Z-spun handspun wool, natural white and brown, indigo blue, and salmon pink probably recarded and respun. Also three-ply, Z-spun, S-twisted commercial yarn, dye unknown, and some two-ply, Z-spun, S-twisted commercial yarn.

Spanish Colonial Arts Society, Inc., Mera Collection, at MNM. L.5.62.80.

Plate 11
Hybrid Style

*B*ands composed of multiple stripes in alternation with plain white zones bearing curious leaf-like units in several combinations of colors form the decorative scheme seen here. Though very similar units have been noted on other blankets of this same class, they do not seem to be referable, at this time, to any other observed style, either Mexican or Indian. From this it would appear that a local invention is probable. Those bands made up entirely of stripes, or the contrary, may be safely assigned to traditional procedure.

All color effects were produced through the use of commercial dyes applied to handspun yarns. There is little doubt but that this blanket was woven during the early 1880s.

Date: 1870s. Size: 87½ by 49 inches. Two widths. Warps: 6 per inch; two-ply, Z-spun, S-twisted handspun wool, white. Wefts: 28 per inch; one-ply, Z-spun handspun wool; natural white and brownish black, and chemically dyed red, pink, purple, and blue.

Spanish Colonial Arts Society, Inc., Mera Collection, at MNM. L.5.62.87.

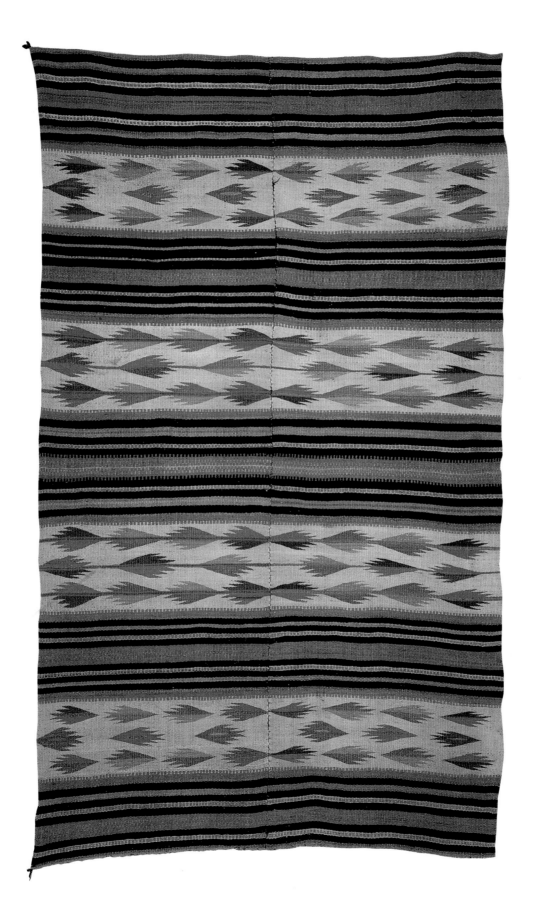

Plate 12
Hybrid Style

A high degree of ornateness characterizes this distinctive piece. It is remarkable in its complexity of design for one of the hybrid group, and it also possesses two features worthy of special attention. In the first place, it is one of those rare examples in which both Mexican and Navajo influences in decoration become about equally important. The Mexican influence is evident in the central diamond-shaped ornament, though in the manner of its treatment there is a suggestion of the Navajo. A replica occupies a position at either end of the blanket. The double row of stepped figures above and below the central panel, each centered by an equal-armed cross, is, on the other hand, pure Navajo design. Despite all this, the overall aspect, due to the way the entire structure of design has been handled, cannot be said to be anything but hybrid Rio Grande in style.

The second point of interest lies in the use of entirely different colors in weaving exactly the same features on opposite halves of the fabric. Such a discrepancy may be seen in the central ornament where the two sections are sewed together. Commercial dyes and handspun yarns were used exclusively.

Date: 1880. Size: 82 by 58 inches. Two widths. Warps: 6 per inch; two-ply, Z-spun, S-twisted handspun wool, white. Wefts: 36 per inch; one-ply, Z-spun handspun wool; natural white and black, natural(?) yellow dye, and chemically dyed red, orange, and purple.

Spanish Colonial Arts Society, Inc., Mera Collection, at MNM. L.5.62.77.

Plate 13
Hybrid Style

*A*lthough differing but little in design from many other blankets falling within the hybrid classification, this specimen has an added interest in being one of the five known examples wherein handspun cotton yarn was incorporated in the weft. In this particular instance, that material was used exclusively for weaving the prominent white bands. All of the various colored sections, on the contrary, are composed of three-ply woolen yarns of the Saxony type. This latter feature indicates a dating not much later than the middle of the 1870s. The scalloped appearance along both edges was probably somewhat less noticeable when the fabric was first taken from the loom, but long usage has tended to compact the cotton, which is less resilient than the wool. The short brownish dashes scattered over the white bands constitute the only link with Mexican tradition.

Date: 1820–1850. Size: 90 by 46 inches. Two widths. Warps: two-ply, Z-spun, S-twisted handspun wool, white. Wefts: one-ply, Z-spun handspun cotton, natural white. Also three-ply, paired, commercial wool yarn, dark indigo, vegetal yellow, cochineal red, and three shades of green. Red dye analyzed by Saltzman.

Collection of the Taylor Museum, 3773.

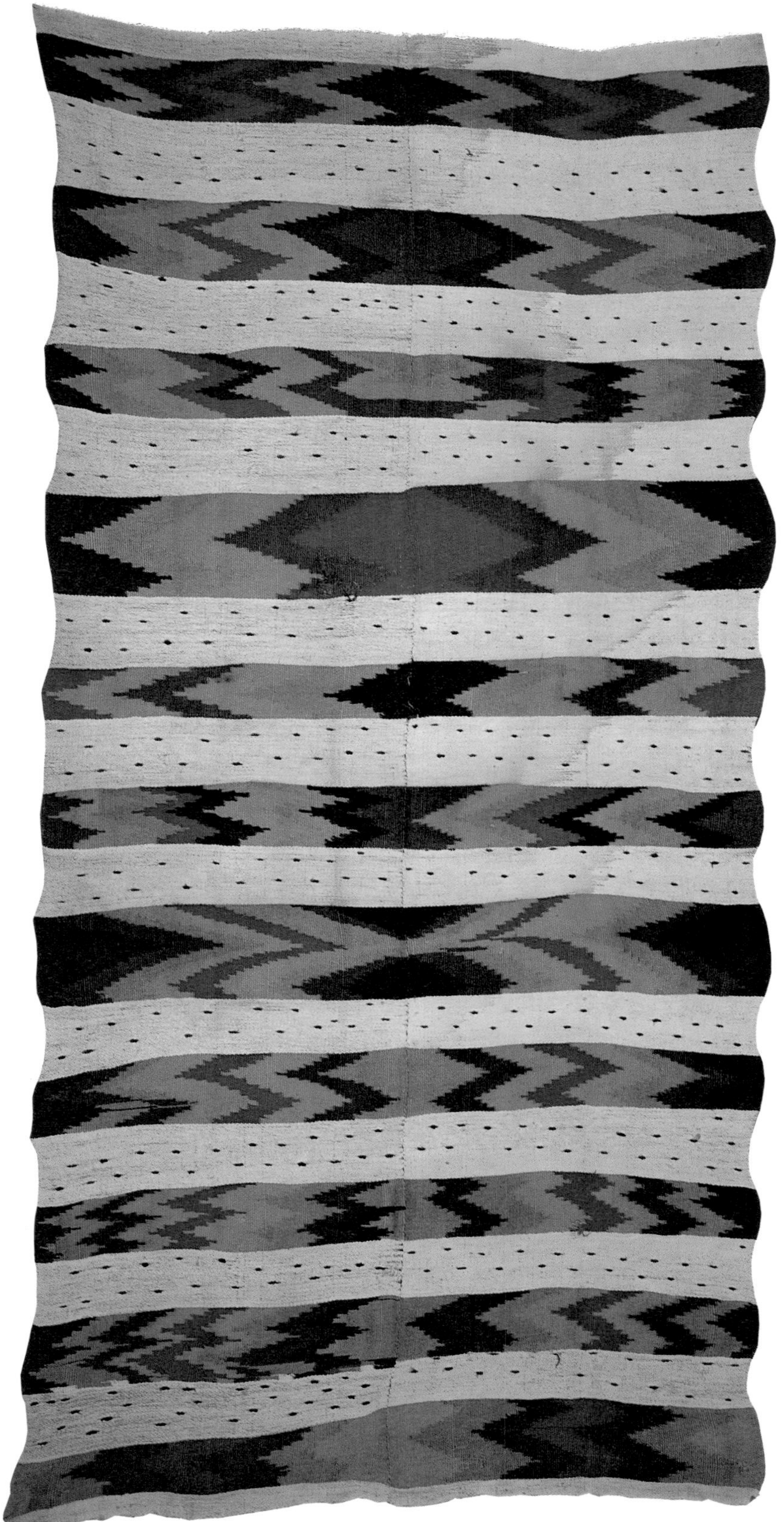

Plate 14
Hybrid Style

*F*rom the fact that Germantown four-ply yarn was used throughout, and also from certain aspects of the decorative treatment, the blanket illustrated here is characterized as one of the latest of the hybrid group. There can be little question but that it was woven when the fully developed Vallero styles (Plates 18 and 19) were in vogue, well into the 1880s. Pseudo-Mexican influence is strongly in evidence, though somewhat modified. If it were not for the absence of the characteristic Vallero eight-pointed star-like device, this blanket would, in most respects, fit nicely within the range of that category.

Date: late 1880s. Size: 78 by 45 inches. Two widths. Warps: 9 per inch; four-ply Germantown, white. Wefts: 40 per inch; four-ply Germantown, chemically dyed red, yellow, lavender, brown, tan, green, and other colors faded to white and gray.

Collections of the Museum of International Folk Art, a unit of the Museum of New Mexico. Gift of Alfred I. Barton. A.65.67.5.

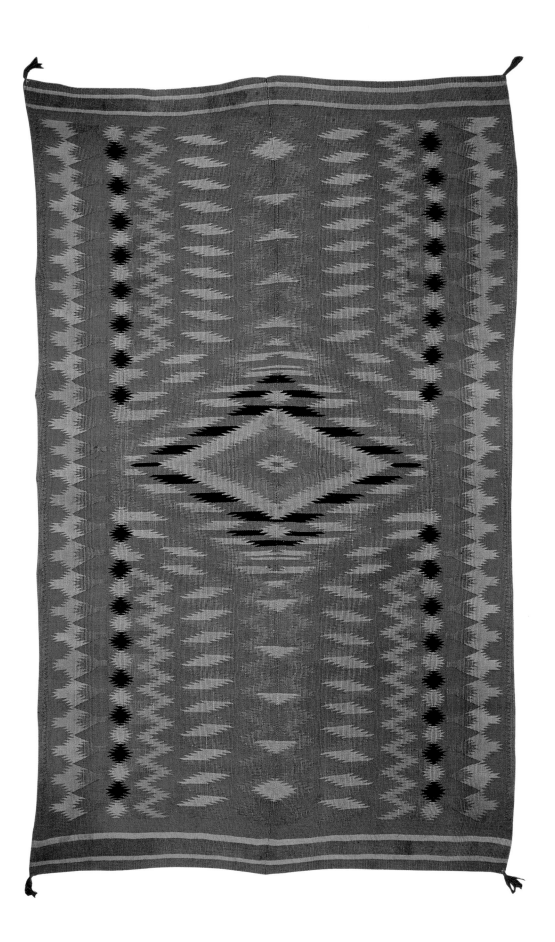

Plate 15
Navajo Copy

*P*ossessing a design that is typically Navajo down to the last detail, this blanket on all other counts is strictly Rio Grande as regards technique. It was woven in two longitudinal sections on a narrow harness loom. Besides such technical matters, the colors, too, are somewhat unusual for the average of Navajo work. There can be no question but that it is plainly a case of direct copying on the part of some Spanish-American craftsman. As is usual for the period between the late 1870s and the earlier years of the 1880s, handspun yarn and commercial dyes are in evidence.

Date: 1880. Size: 82 by 58 inches. Two widths. Warps: 6 per inch; two-ply, Z-spun, S-twisted handspun wool, white. Wefts: 36 per inch; one-ply handspun wool, Z-spun wool; natural brown and chemically dyed reds, orange, and turquoise.

Spanish Colonial Arts Society, Inc., Mera Collection, at MNM. L.5.62.79.

Plate 16
Navajo Copy

*A*nother copy of a Navajo blanket appears here but with a decorative treatment representative of a totally different style period from that seen on the preceding plate. The three prominent lozenge-shaped areas, though perhaps remotely of Mexican derivation, have been treated to conform so thoroughly to the general scheme of decoration accorded the other portions of the blanket, that any of their original significance seems to have been utterly lost. If it were not for technical details in weaving, this specimen, as far as design is concerned, could well be taken for a product of some Navajo weaver. Handspun yarns colored with commercial dyes were exclusively employed.

Date: 1870s. Size: 79 by 46½ inches. Two widths. Warps: 7 per inch; two-ply, Z-spun, S-twisted handspun wool, along with one-ply white and one-ply natural brown. Wefts: 40 per inch; one-ply, Z-spun handspun wool; natural white and brown and chemically dyed orange, turquoise, magenta, red, and purple.

Spanish Colonial Arts Society, Inc., Mera Collection, at MNM. L.5.62.65.

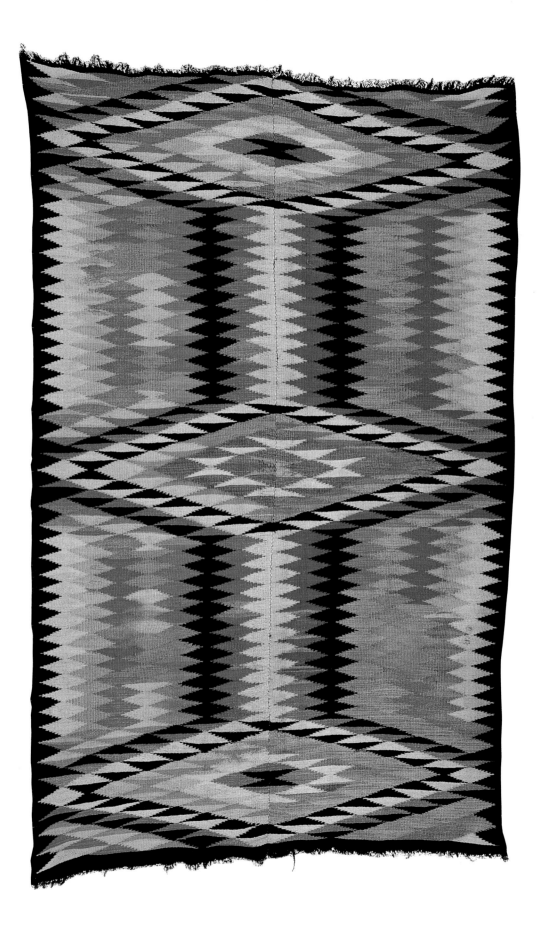

Plate 17
Vallero Style

*T*his rather flamboyant specimen of the Spanish-American weaver's art is notable for its unusually intricate pattern. It also has the distinction of being, as far as is known, the earliest example in which an eight-pointed, star-like device has been incorporated into the design. This figure is the distinguishing mark of a specialization known as the Vallero style.

An estimate of the age of this blanket becomes possible on the basis of the kind of materials used. Besides a handspun warp, only three-ply commercial yarns entered into the weft structure. Because it is known from collateral information that yarns such as these became largely unavailable after about the middle of the 1870s, an approximate idea of age is obtained. All other recorded examples of the Vallero type, except for some manifestly late handspun copies, were woven entirely of a later four-ply type of material. As may be seen, the basic scheme of decoration is clearly pseudo-Mexican.

Date: 1870s. Size: 84 by 48 inches. Two widths. Warps: 9 per inch; two-ply, Z-spun, S-twisted handspun wool, white. Wefts: 48 per inch; one-ply, Z-spun handspun wool, natural white. Also three-ply commercial wool, chemically dyed red, brownish red, dark blue, orange, and green; and four-ply commercial wool, chemically dyed light blue, yellow, and purple.

International Folk Art Foundation Collection at the Museum of International Folk Art, a unit of the Museum of New Mexico. Gift of the Fred Harvey Fine Arts Collection. L.70.3.39 = new number FA.79.64.95.

Plate 18
Vallero Style

*A*lso conforming in the larger features to the pseudo-Mexican idea is this blanket of the Vallero class. In this instance, as well as for a majority of this group, all the weaving elements consist of commercial four-ply yarn, often generalized under the name Germantown. Because of this, a period in the 1880s, or perhaps slightly later, has been assigned for this sort. In connection with the eight-pointed Vallero star, it may be of interest to know that a study of the subject has not yet disclosed a satisfactory origin for this figure, nor has it been found on any other Southwestern or Mexican textile dating from a time prior to its appearance on the Vallero type.

Date: 1880s. Size: 85 by 40 inches. Two widths. Warps: 9 per inch; two-ply, Z-spun, S-twisted handspun wool, white. Wefts: 36 per inch; one-ply, Z-spun handspun wool, natural white. Also four-ply, chemically dyed red, yellow, orange, light blue, light green, and turquoise green.

Spanish Colonial Arts Society, Inc., Mera Collection, at MNM. L.5.62.76.

Plate 19
Vallero Style

*T*he weaver of this greatly modified member of the Vallero group has retained but little of the pseudo-Mexican tradition in planning an all-over design. Only a simplification of the usually elaborately treated borders suggests any relationship with that style. It may have been thought that a greater number of stars would compensate for a less complexly designed field. Here again, as in the blanket just discussed, a commercial four-ply material (Germantown) has been employed, a fact which would tend to indicate a like period of manufacture for both.

Date: 1880s. Size: 80 by 47 inches. Warps: 11 per inch. Wefts: 36 per inch.

School of American Research Collections in the Museum of New Mexico, Laboratory of Anthropology, 9506/12.

Plate 20
Utility Blanket

The production of an indifferent to poor grade of common utility blanket continued without interruption from the inception of harness-loom weaving in the colonies for well over one hundred and fifty years. This sort was first designated in old documents as ''coarse,'' ''camp,'' and ''patio.'' The example figured here is of comparatively late weave, wherein a thick handspun yarn, dyed with aniline colors, was used. In later years, such heavy fabrics were quite popular for use as lap-robes and for camp beds.

It is more than probable that if all the Rio Grande harness-loom blankets produced since the beginning could be known, the utility type would outnumber the finer weaves as much as a hundred to one.

Size: 82 by 44 inches.

Private collection.

Plate 21
Chimayo Blanket

A typical specimen of the true Chimayo blanket is illustrated here. The group of which this is a member should be considered as merely constituting another subdivision under the more general heading of Rio Grande blanketry, rather than as anything in the nature of a separate development. This is true in spite of the employment of a decorative system entirely distinct from that of any other subclass in the larger classification. Although the designs differ so radically from anything previously seen, it must be remembered that the same simple form of loom was used and that some of the same artisans, in the beginning of the style, must have produced, to some extent, both the old and new forms concurrently. Just who was responsible for inventing such a bizarre decorative fashion will probably never be definitely known. Germantown four-ply yarn has always been utilized in weaving this sort.

Size: 72 by 48 inches.

Private collection.

Plate 22
Chimayo Blanket

*I*n order to demonstrate further the peculiarities of Chimayo ideas on decorative forms, another example of that type is shown here. The remarks concerning material and other matters made in connection with the previously figured specimen are equally pertinent here. However, in addition it should be pointed out that, though the technique of weaving remained unaltered, looms capable of handling widths equal to those of the present-day blanket eventually superseded the older, narrower models when a fabric of large size was desired. Such a change appears to have occurred with the appearance of the true Chimayo type.

Size: 72 by 48 inches.

Private collection.

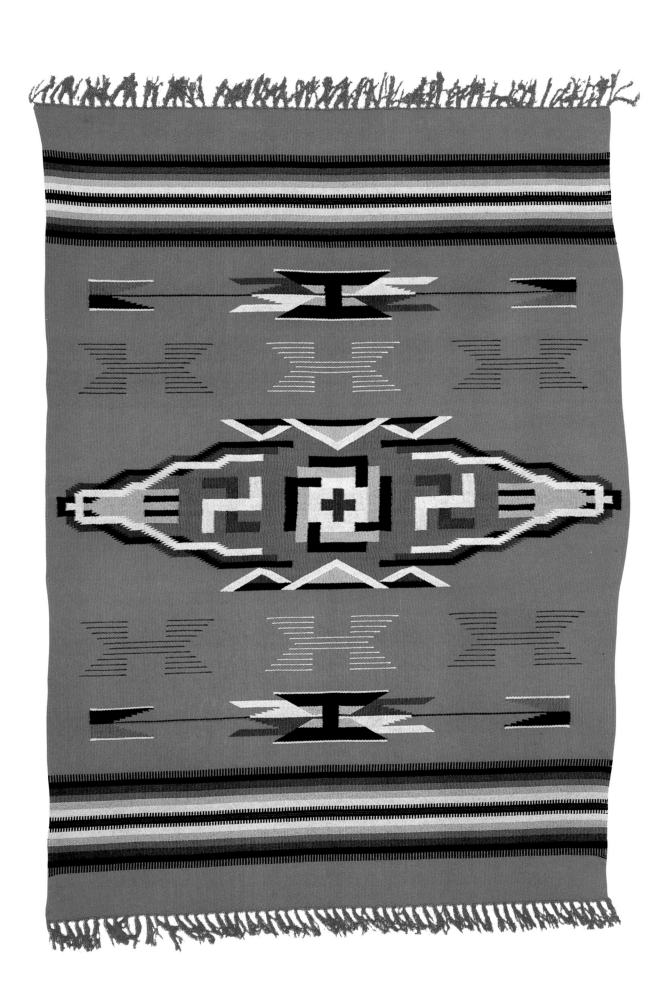

Plate 23
"Revival" Blanket

The blanket pictured here was woven around 1920, during one of the sporadic attempts to revive the use of handspun yarns for the looming of Chimayo textiles. Like a number of similar trials, the effort was abandoned for financial reasons.

This piece is most unusual because no dyeing of any of the material was involved. The black is that obtained from black sheep. All of the lighter shades of grayish brown were made by carding together varying proportions of white wool with natural black.

The only feature of design, except for the striping, that would definitely link with the past is the lozenge-shaped ornament located in the center. Two rows of figures formed by a vertical series of horizontal lines, a not unusual arrangement in Chimayo designing, are of secondary interest. Other figures of this sort, executed in a like manner, may be seen on Plate 22, above and below the central decorative composition. Although all of the weft elements are handspun, the warp is of four-ply commercial yarn.

Size: 82 by 38 inches.

Private collection.

Plate 24
"Revival" Blanket

A final phase, or perhaps incident might be a more descriptive term, took place in the history of Rio Grande blanket weaving some fifteen years ago. This was the result of an attempt by certain weavers to produce something less fantastic in design and conservative in color, more in the spirit of the old order. Unfortunately, this move never reached any particular degree of popularity, and the effort was soon abandoned. An example of this so-called "revival" type is illustrated here. In this, although the general character and treatment of the simply striped portions adequately reflect traditional fashions, the designer has introduced other stripes composed of rhomboidal elements, a treatment more characteristic for Navajo textiles. A fine grade of four-ply commmercial yarn was employed in weaving this variety.

Size: 76 by 48 inches.

Private collection.